THE KINGDOM MOMENT
31-Day Devotional

MICHAEL T. JAMES

Copyright © 2016 by MICHAEL T. JAMES

THE KINGDOM MOMENT
31-Day Devotional
by MICHAEL T. JAMES

Printed in the United States of America.

ISBN 9781498466172

All rights reserved solely by the author. The author guarantees all contents are original and do not infringe upon the legal rights of any other person or work. No part of this book may be reproduced in any form without the permission of the author. The views expressed in this book are not necessarily those of the publisher.

Scripture quotations taken from the New King James Version (NKJV). Copyright © 1982 by Thomas Nelson, Inc. Used by permission. All rights reserved.

www.xulonpress.com

DEDICATED TO THE FOLLOWING:

To the late Christopher Price, my beloved parents, the late William and Alice James. To my wife Tanya James: thank you for the encouragement and continued belief in this monthly devotional and me.

INTRODUCTION
By Pastor Michael T. James

According to Genesis 1:26-28, God created mankind in His image and likeness. Mankind was blessed by God and given the mandate of dominion. It was God's original intent for mankind to rule the earth as His Kingdom representative in the exact same manner as God ruled the heavens.

Adam and Eve forfeited their right and privilege as rulers on the earth when they willfully disobeyed God. Man's authority was transferred to Satan. In the fullness of time, Jesus Christ came from God as God in the human form in order to reestablish the Kingdom of God as a present day reality in the earth.

The first message declared by Jesus Christ is recorded in Matthew 4:17: "Repent, for the Kingdom of Heaven is at hand." The word "repent" means to change one's mind and to think differently.

This 31-day devotional, *The Kingdom Moment*, has been created to help you discover some key spiritual truths about the Kingdom of God. It will help you build a solid foundation on the different dimensions of the Kingdom of God such as healing, dominion, sonship, salvation, praise, authority, and purpose. You will discover how to live a Kingdom-focused life as personified in the life of Jesus Christ.

Remember, you were created to rule and reign in every area of your life in this life *now,* not only in the life to come. Get ready for a wonderful journey and know the Kingdom of God has already come.

Let's get started!

WEEK 1
DAYS 1-7

"The Priority of the Kingdom of God"

Day 1

Establishing the Kingdom

"Your Kingdom come, Your will be done on earth as it is in heaven." —Matthew 6:10

It is the entire purpose of God for His Kingdom to be established in the earth *now* as a present-day reality. Many of us possess a "rapture ready" mentality, and we believe we have to wait to experience God's Kingdom in the future after we die. There is no need to wait until later when God desires His Kingdom here on earth to be like it is in heaven.

What does it mean to establish the Kingdom? It means to release the rule, reign, royal power, authority, and dominion of God in the hearts of people. When we acknowledge and submit to the King in our hearts, then the Kingdom of God will manifest in us.

In this verse, Jesus Christ provides insight on establishing the Kingdom. Christ shares with His disciples the manner on how to pray to the Father. Unfortunately, many of us have labeled this as the Lord's Prayer; however, it is a model on how we are to pray. He gives us the components of our prayers. We have a great and awesome opportunity to commune with our Heavenly Father on a daily basis.

Christ teaches us we are to open our prayer with adoration to the Father, "Our Father in heaven, hallowed be thy name." Secondly, we are to pray God's Kingdom to come, which is His will to be on earth as it is in heaven. The word "is" lets us know it is the purpose of God to be established on the earth as it is already in heaven. The word "is" is present tense. In heaven where God dwells at this very moment, there is not any sickness, disease, poverty, lack, wickedness, evil, hatred, racism, greed, sexism, doubt, fear, or the devil.

What should we pray to God? We need to shift our prayer focus to establishing His Kingdom, and we will see awesome results. Let us bring the Kingdom to the earth now. We have a guarantee from Christ Himself, if we seek His Kingdom first and His righteousness, then all the things we need in life will be granted to us!

Day 2

God is Thinking About You

> *"'For I know the thoughts that I think toward you,' says the Lord, 'thoughts of peace and not of evil, to give you a future and a hope.'" —Jeremiah 29:11*

There are several attributes that describe God. He is omnipresent, omnipotent, and omniscient. As an all-knowing God, there is not anything we can experience or go through God does not already know. In fact, God knows every detail about our lives—including our ending, the beginning, and all that happens in between.

When we understand our days upon this earth are already fashioned by God, we will live with great expectations. This means God has already gone before us, cleared out the way, and provided for us everything we need in life before we were born. With God as the supreme being of love, we are forever on the mind of God. At this moment, God is thinking about you. The mere fact He is thinking about us brings a smile to the face of God and should also bring a smile to our faces.

In this verse, the prophet Jeremiah is told by God to instruct the nation of Israel that He has good thoughts about them, not evil thoughts. In addition, He has great plans for them and to bring them to a great future. It is easy to be fearful and anxious about the future. We can enjoy life to the fullest when we understand the purposes of God for our lives. As we embrace His plans, we will experience total completeness in life. Be encouraged and excited about your future. Why? God is thinking about you.

Day 3
Push Forward

> *"For His anger is but for a moment, His favor is for life;*
> *Weeping endure for a night, but joy comes in the morning."*
> —*Psalm 30:5*

In life, we can be assured we will encounter seasons of difficulties, where during these difficulties, we have natural inclinations to quit or forfeit. Truth be told, we are actually a few moments away from our breakthroughs and don't know it. It is for this reason we must push forward to experience the *best* life God has ordained for us.

What does "weeping endures for a night" mean (as stated in Psalm 30:5)? It means a time of extreme grief, sorrow, and sadness. To weep is a natural and common emotion, which allows a release. Weeping, in itself is not the problem, but becomes the problem when we allow it to stop us from pushing forward. It is a brief and difficult time during a trial, but we can be assured a new day is coming. At 12:01 a.m. each day, a new day begins, even though it is still dark outside. Midnight is a dimension of transition, for we are being shifted into a new day.

In this verse from Psalm 30, the psalmist, who is King David, states how to handle a personal time of difficulty. He was the second king of Israel, but David was also a warrior and a worshipper. For Christians, with all the devastating news we hear on a daily basis, we must remain vigilant with steadfastness and fight through the storms of life as warriors. In addition, at the same time, we must be worshippers. A true worshipper is a person who acknowledges the worth of God, no matter what he or she has or doesn't have.

In Psalm 30:5, David was delivered by God from some trial, realizing after the weeping and enduring that joy would come into his life. After trials, it is time to embrace your joy and be content in your situation. In God's presence, there is fullness of joy and at His right hand, pleasures evermore. There is nothing wrong to weep for a moment, but prepare to receive God's favor for life.

Day 4

No Condemnation

"There is therefore now no condemnation to those who are in Christ Jesus." —Romans 8:1

One of the greatest hindrances to living a Kingdom-focused life is we are plagued by our past mistakes, decisions, and failures. We will never enjoy the present or look with expectation for the future when we live in the past.

Many people believe we are made righteous with God because of what we do. However, none of us are able to live good enough to keep the laws of God. We are only made righteous when we place our belief in Jesus Christ and rest in His finished work. The great news about the love of God is He loves us fully without condemnation.

What does condemnation mean? It means damnatory sentence, to be found guilty, and to receive judgment with punishment when a law is broken. [1] Unfortunately, all of us deserve God's judgment because we fail and break His laws on a daily basis.

In this verse, the Apostle Paul shares with the believers at the church in Rome how they are free from condemnation. The Apostle tells them and the same is true for us today—we are free from condemnation because of the price Jesus Christ paid on the cross by shedding His blood. In fact, we are forever forgiven for all of our sins: past, present, and future. Paul tells us we have no damnatory sentence with judgment because of our relationship with Jesus

---

[1] https://www.blueletterbible.org/kjv/rom/8/1/ss1/s_1054001

Christ. So today, make a decision to walk in the fullness of life because God says we are not guilty!

Day 5
New Mercies

"Through the Lord's mercies, we are not consumed, because His compassions fail not. They are new every morning, great is your faithfulness." —Lamentations 3:22-23

There is a fundamental truth we must understand: none of us are able to live good enough to please God. If we truly understood the mercies of God, we would be inspired to have a greater commitment to God's purposes for our lives. Every time we sin and miss the mark, we deserve death, but thanks be to God, He releases new mercies to us on a daily basis.

In this verse, the prophet Jeremiah writes to the nation of Israel to explain the reality of God's mercy. As a whole, the nation of Israel had turned away from following God. For this reason, God permitted His chosen people to be overrun by their enemies for a certain season. They had been taken hostage in captivity. In the process of time, Jeremiah was encouraged when he personally began to remember God's faithfulness and goodness.

It does not matter what our current situation is today; we need to be mindful of God's faithfulness, goodness, and divine favor. As we remember, we are able to endure the hardships, adversity, and trials in life. Sometimes, we may find ourselves in a desperate situation, but we are not in a hopeless situation. It is time for us to rejoice, be glad, rest, and receive the new mercies of God.

Day 6
Count It All Joy

"My brethren, count it all joy when you fall into various trials, knowing that the testing of your faith produces patience." —James 1:2-3

As we walk with God in the Kingdom, there will be seasons in our lives when we experience trials and tests. Many of us do not like these difficult seasons. We often want God to immediately remove us from the trials. Just because we are saved does not mean we will be exempt from trials and tests.

In this verse, James, the half-brother of Jesus, writes to the scattered twelve tribes to encourage them. They underwent a severe season of testing with trials on every hand. He tells them and reminds us in the midst of our seasons of testing with trials, we are to count it all joy. This means we are to consider what we experience with cheerfulness. We are to smile in the midst of the trial.

We must remember God is in control of our trials. He does not send or cause them, but may permit them for a greater purpose. God is the acting supervisor of the trials we face. He knows why the trials are permitted, how long the trials will last, what we should learn while we are in the trial, when we will come out of the trial, and what is on the other side of the trial.

The larger the trial, the larger the blessing we will receive after the trial. We should be encouraged to know trials do not always last. Let us embrace our trials today with a smile.

Day 7
Perfect Peace

"You will keep him in perfect peace, whose mind is stayed on You, because he trusts in you. —Isaiah 26:3

One of the greatest needs in our lives is peace. It is important for us to grasp it is the will of God for us to experience peace in every area of our lives.

During the difficult times, it is easy for us to live with anxiety. Anxiety is the result of an absence of peace. Paul tells us in Philippians 4:6, "be anxious for nothing, but in all things by prayer and supplication with thanksgiving." It is time for us to be mindful of the favor God has released in our lives. It is this peace of God, which will invade our spirits when we pause, praise, and give thanks to God in everything.

In this verse, the prophet Isaiah writes to the nation of Israel to encourage them as God prepared to move them into a new season. What is "perfect peace"? This verse is actually translated, as God guards your mind, He will give you peace when you confidently and completely lean upon God. We have many things we have leaned on in the past and even in this moment, but we will never receive the peace of God. We will experience perfect peace when we solely trust God and have a steadfast mind.

We must always be encouraged and know God is a keeper. May our Heavenly Father grant you peace—peace in our minds, bodies, careers, communities, churches, and in all of our relationships. Do not permit the current conditions of life to keep you in pieces, but remember the Prince of Peace. Let us keep our minds on Christ and receive His peace!

WEEKLY DEVOTIONAL REFLECTION QUESTIONS

1. What were the major spiritual truths revealed to you this week?
2. What spiritual truths and/or principles can you apply to your spiritual life from this week's devotions?
3. How do you plan to share the spiritual truths and/or principles with others around you?

WEEK 2
DAYS 8-14

"The Power of the *Word* of God"

Day 8

The Love of God

> *"For God so loved the world that He gave His only begotten Son, that whoever believes in Him should not perish but have everlasting life."* —John 3:16

One of our greatest needs in life is to be loved and give love to others. Many of us may not have received the love of God. When we truly receive the love of God, many of relationship's challenges would cease. The attitude, nature, and character of God are love. God is the perfect picture of unconditional love. God loves with *agape* love. The word *agape* refers to a deep and constant love and interest of a perfect Being toward entirely unworthy objects. [2]

There is nothing we can ever do to make God stop loving us. There is no greater demonstration of God's love toward us than the gift of His Son, Jesus Christ, who was born to die on the cross for our sins and be raised from the dead.

In this verse, a Pharisee named Nicodemus visited Jesus Christ. Nicodemus came to Christ at night. He was a ruler of the Jews and acknowledged Christ as a great teacher, but failed to acknowledge Him as God's Son and Savior of the world. It is a spirit of religion that hinders us from receiving the love of God.

Jesus told Nicodemus, "unless a man is born again, he [could] not enter into the Kingdom of God." What is the revelation? Jesus actually said unless we leave the program of organized religion and

---

[2] https://www.blueletterbible.org/kjv/jhn/3/16/ss1/s_1000016

embrace the program of the Kingdom, we would never experience a spiritual rebirth and enter into a personal relationship with Him. Jesus Christ is the personification of God's love toward us. We do not have to work for this love because it is completely free and without condemnation. Be encouraged today and know we are so loved. The time has come for us to receive God's love and live the *best* life!

Day 9

The Word is Settled

> *"Forever, O Lord, Your word is settled in heaven."*
> *—Psalm 119:89*

Everything that exists in the visible and invisible worlds was framed by the word of God. We have a guarantee that heaven and earth will pass away, but the word of God will remain forever. Each of us is a "word" from God. We were created by the word of God in eternity and were released in time to be born into a certain family with a Kingdom purpose. At the end of our lives, we will return to eternity as a word, completing all God had assigned to us to do.

Whether we realize it or not, everything about our lives is already forever settled in heaven. Unfortunately, our problem is we have actually forgotten what God declared about us and has purposed for us. What does "the word is settled" mean? It simply means every word spoken, declared, and commanded by our Heavenly Father is already fixed and established in heaven. The words spoken by God are already declared and cannot be changed, altered, rearranged, or prevented.

In this verse, the Psalmist provides us with insight to God's faithfulness especially as it pertains to His word. This is the longest chapter in the Bible, and this Psalm is known as the "Word Psalm." The Psalmist reminds us we can look at the stability of the universe and the word of God at work. The word of God is permanent, and all that He has created in the universe serves Him. As a word from God, we were created to serve Him. All we have, all we do, and will do is for one purpose: to serve Him.

There is only true way to serve the Lord: agree with Him. We are to be in accord, in sync, and in harmony with His word. When we disagree with the word, it means we actually doubt His word. God's word says we are blessed; we are the head and not the tail; we are lenders and not borrowers; and we need to fully agree with every word spoken by God. If God says it, we believe it, that settles it, and we can achieve it. The word is forever fixed, and we cannot do anything about it except agree with it!

Day 10

A Break in the Family Line

> *"And Jabez called on the name of God of Israel saying, 'Oh, that you would bless me indeed and enlarge my territory that Your hand would be with me, and that You would keep me from evil, that I may not cause pain!' So God granted him what he had requested."* —1 Chronicles 4:10

All of us were placed in an earthly family. For those of us who are saved by Jesus Christ, we have also been placed into God's family. Every person born into a family starts at the same level. The circumstances that exist in a family are often due to the choices made by the family members. Your life today is the result of your choices. In order to change your life, you must change your choices.

If we want to live our *best* life, we must have a personal revelation of who God is and then enter into a relationship with Him no matter what any other family member does. If we don't know our family's history, we may be doomed to repeat it.

In this verse, a man named Jabez provides insight on how to become the break in the family line. His name translates as, "pain."[3] Can you imagine being called "pain"? He was more honorable than all of his brothers. Jabez teaches us we may have been born into a painful situation, but we must refuse to answer to names and labels

---

[3] https://www.blueletterbible.org/kjv/1ch/4/10/ss1/s_342010

we are not. We have not been created to live a life of average and tolerate mediocrity, but live a life based on what God has ordained.

Many of us lack the revelation of God because we don't know what God has promised to us in His Word. We perish because of a lack of knowledge. Jabez cried out to God and sought a relationship with the covenant God of his fathers. He boldly prayed to God and told Him he wanted to be blessed, enlarge his territory, protect him from the evil one, and not cause Him pain. What did God do? He granted Jabez all that he requested. God gave to him because of His grace and favor. We have not because we ask not. Be bold today and ask God for the *best* life and prepare to live it!

Day 11

Who Will You Believe?

> *"And they gave the children of Israel a bad report of the land which they spied out, saying, 'The land through which we have gone as spies is a land that devours its inhabitants, and all the people who whom we saw in it are men of great stature.'"* —Numbers 13:32

One quality we should desire in our close friends is to trust their word. Our ability to trust a person is based upon our relationship and experiences we have had with them. Unfortunately, there are some people we cannot trust because of their inability to keep their word. However, our Heavenly Father is the only One who will be completely true to His Word. Since God said it, that settles it, we believe it, and we receive it by faith. Who and what we choose to believe will either impact our lives for the better or worse.

God will never let us down, and we can completely and confidently place our full trust in Him.

In this verse, the nation of Israel made a wrong choice to believe the bad report of ten spies rather than to embrace and trust the Word of God. God permitted Moses to choose twelve spies to be sent out and to survey the Promised Land. After a period of forty days, the twelve spies returned with evidence of some of the fruit in the land and shared their results with the rest of people. In short, the spies confessed the land was exactly like God had told them.

It flowed with milk and honey, but the ten of the spies also told them the people in the land were like giants and devoured their inhabitants. An entire nation of Israel, except Caleb and Joshua, chose to believe the bad report of the ten spies rather than God. Due to this bad report, a great number of people missed their destiny and died in the wilderness, even though they were on the brink of the Promised Land. The remainder of the people had to wait another forty years to experience what God had already given them. Unbelief will always cause us to miss the manifestation of the promises of God.

We must be careful whom we allow to speak and what words are spoken into our lives. We must choose be in a relationship with people who will confirm the Word that God has already given and agree with His Word. Who will you believe? We must choose God at His Word.

Day 12

Complete Trust

"It is better to trust in the Lord rather than to put confidence in man." —Psalm 118:8

We have a tendency to over trust man and to under trust God. There are 1188 chapters in the Bible, and this Psalm is in the direct middle of the Bible and contains a powerful revelation. As believers, it is imperative for us to have complete trust in the Lord As we look at the heart and character of God, we know He can fully be trusted.

In this verse, the Psalmist makes it clear whom we are to place our trust in and whom we are not to trust. This psalm is a collection of psalms known as the "Egyptian Praise" because these psalms spoke about the salvation that began in Israel's exodus from Egypt. The Psalmist reminds us that it is good and pleasant for us to place our trust in the Lord than to trust or feel safe in man. The Hebrew word for Lord is the "Existing One who is immutable and has all authority."[4] This is the primary reason we can trust God is He is unchanging with all authority. Things and people around us may shake, fall, fail, and change, but Jesus Christ is the same-yesterday, today, and forever.

---

[4] https://www.blueletterbible.org/lang/Lexicon/Lexicon.cfm?strongs=H3068&t=KJV

We must stop being fearful, timid, and afraid of uncertainty in this world, but we must learn to agree with God and His Word. Let's trust Him even when we cannot trace Him!

Day 13

Saved By Grace

> *"For by grace you have been saved through faith, and that not of yourselves; it is the gift of God, not of works, lest any man should boast." —Ephesians 2:8*

Many of us don't fully understand what it means to be saved by grace. The gift of salvation is available for all to experience; however, it simply requires a decision to accept Jesus Christ as one's Lord and Savior by faith. Salvation for mankind is free because Jesus Christ paid a great price!

To be saved by grace means God has granted us His grace in order for us to place our confidence and trust in Jesus Christ as our Lord and Savior. We don't deserve salvation due to our sinful nature, but God provided an opportunity for salvation through our faith in Jesus Christ alone and not by our good works.

In this verse, the Apostle Paul shares with us how salvation works. He penned this epistle to the Ephesian church and reminded them they had been saved by grace. They had not obtained salvation because of their works, but solely by the grace of God. Faith is the channel and not the cause. God alone saves. Paul reminded them salvation never originated in the efforts of people, but it arose out of the loving kindness of God. It is a great blessing to be saved. Truly, salvation is of the Lord.

As believers, our salvation occurred in the past at the Cross. We must remember we cannot do any works to earn our salvation.

Everything that we receive in our lives is a gift from our merciful and gracious Father. Salvation has its privileges, and it is time for us to fully exercise them.

Day 14

Faultless

> *"Now to Him who is able to keep you from stumbling, and to present you faultless before the presence of His glory with exceeding joy, to God, our Savior, who alone is wise, be glory, dominion, and power, both now and forever. Amen."* —Jude 24-25

Due to the finished work of Jesus Christ on the Cross, we are considered faultless in the eyes of our Heavenly Father. In our world today, it is easy to find and place fault on others. To find fault means to seek and make known one's flaws or defects. Fault-finding is a daily occurrence—whether it is in politics, entertainment, sports, education, business, families, and even in the body of Christ.

The Word of God tells us in John 8:7 he without sin casts the first stone. None of us possess the moral ability to judge and to condemn others. The reason we can boldly declare we are faultless is because of the blood of Jesus Christ covers all our sins: past, present, and future. For those of us who have accepted the King in our lives as Lord and Savior, we are considered faultless.

In these verses, Jude summed up what it meant to be faultless and why we are faultless. Jude provides us on how to stand fast in the grace and the truth of Jesus Christ. Many false teachers had come against the truth of Jesus Christ. He admonished the believers to focus on their faith in God and not be consumed with the faultfinders.

The Kingdom Moment

In this benediction, Jude concluded his letter with exuberant praise for the Lord, who alone would keep believers from being deceived.

He spoke to the person, power, and purpose for our being faultless. The reason we are faultless is because of God, who is able, who has the capacity, who has the strength and the power to watch over us. In addition, He is the one who causes us to stand without blemish. As a matter of fact, we are considered "perfect" because of Christ.

Our response to being faultless is to praise Jesus Christ, who is the author and the finisher of our faith. The next time you are criticized and condemned wrongly by others, remember one word: "faultless."

WEEKLY DEVOTIONAL REFLECTION QUESTIONS

1. What were the major spiritual truths revealed to you during this week?
2. What spiritual truths and/or principles can you apply to your spiritual life from this week's devotions?
3. How do you plan to share the spiritual truths and/or principles with others around you?

WEEK 3
DAYS 15-21

"Strength for Life's Journey"

Day 15

A Very Present Help

> *"God is our refuge and strength, a very present help in trouble."* —Psalm 46:10

In pursuit of the abundant life, we can expect to encounter seasons of trials and trouble. Often unknown to us, God permits trials and trouble. We cannot always control what happens to us, but we can control our responses. Our responses should not be to lose our heads and become fearful and frustrated. The proper response should be, "Lord, I thank you because you trust me with this trouble, and I know you are with me in spite of the trouble."

The phrase "a very present help" means during the time of distress and straits, we will receive the exceeding assistance and aid we need at the moment we need it. God is the assistance and aid we need during our seasons of trials and trouble.

In this verse, the Psalmist has provided us with a picture of how God Himself is our very present help. This psalm is a "psalm of trust." The Psalmist rejoiced in the deliverance that the Lord had given to His people in the midst of a fearsome battle or siege. When the adversary brings trouble into our lives, God raises the standard. God is our refuge and shelter in the midst of trouble. He is our defense. God is the very present help we need when we need it.

God will never be late or too early during the difficult seasons of life. The songwriter says He is an on-time God. It does not matter what current trials and troubles we face. We have a guarantee our

God will be present now with us and be the refreshing aid we need. Not only should we praise God for the trouble, but we should also rest in Him during the trouble. He is only a praise and prayer away. God is always on time!

Day 16

Don't Quit Now

"But Jesus said to him, 'No one having his hand put to the plow, and looking back is fit the Kingdom of God.'" — Luke 9:62

There is a natural tendency for us to quit when a task becomes difficult. Even believers are not exempt from challenges in life. As a matter of fact, Jesus Christ has told us John 16:33 in the Word of God, "in this life, we will have tribulation, but be of good cheer and I know I have already overcome them." Whatever we face in life, we have the full assurance Jesus Christ has already gone before us and also have overcome whatever we will face.

Many believers have forfeited and quit their dreams. Whether the dream is to pursue a college career, write a book, start a new business, or seek after a promotion and advancement in their jobs. A winner never quits, and a quitter never wins.

In this verse, Jesus Christ told an important spiritual truth of not quitting, especially when it comes to our pursuit of a Kingdom-focused life. On this particular journey, Christ encountered a person and told him to follow Him wherever He went. Like many of us, this man hastily responded without considering the costs to follow Christ. A true Kingdom-focused life requires a commitment to discipleship.

In Luke 9:60-62, Christ provides a description of the commitment needed for true discipleship. The aspiring man told Christ, "I will follow you," after he went home to bury his father.

Jesus, in His love and wisdom, said, "Let the dead bury the dead." He also said, "Another man is not fit for the Kingdom if he puts his hand to plow and looks back."

What did Jesus mean? Jesus told the man and therefore tells us that we are not ready for use in divine service if we are not completely serious in this commitment. Putting a hand to plow symbolizes engagement in a task. This task Jesus referred to is our serving in the Kingdom of God. We will never be able to progress and advance in life with a tendency of always looking back.

If we continue to look back, we will never fully walk in our God-ordained destinies. Jesus Christ does not want us to be lukewarm in our service to Him. Don't quit now because we are closer than we have ever been!

Day 17
All Things

"And we know that all things work together for good to those who love God, to those who are called according to His purpose." —Romans 8:28

There is a misperception within the body of Christ about the sovereignty of God. What is the sovereignty of God? It is His absolute right to do all things according to His own good pleasure. All the things we have experienced in our lives up to this moment have been permitted by the sovereignty of God.

It is contrary to the nature and character of God to send evil and destructive things into our lives. God is not the sender of earthquakes, hurricanes, tornadoes, mudslides, disease, destruction, or death. God is a loving, kind, merciful, and gracious Father, but may permit evil things to occur. Many of us struggle to find purpose in our lives because of what we may have experienced in the past. No matter what has happened in our past, all things may not have been good for us, but they will work together for our good. God wants the glory no matter what our story may be.

In this verse, the Apostle Paul is writing to the believers in Rome. He wanted them to know even in their present circumstances of suffering, God worked things together for their good. God often permits us to experience "suffering seasons" so we solely rely upon Jesus Christ for our strength, stability, and sustainment. Paul told them all things would work together in cooperation for their benefit because they loved God, and they had been called according to God's purpose. All things do not work together for good for unbelievers who live in the world. Unfortunately for them, these things are evil things that happen to them. Our love is the response to the work of the Holy Ghost in us when bad things happen to us.

Our Heavenly Father permits everything in our lives in order to accomplish His overarching plan. As believers, we need to embrace our all things no matter how large or small, good or bad. We must not allow our past to prevent us from experiencing all God has ordained for us. Let's change our perception and see the purpose and value of all things. We are greatly loved by the Father, and He has a magnificent Kingdom purpose for us.

Day 18

Pursue, Overtake, and Recover All

> *"So David inquired of the Lord, saying, 'Shall I pursue this troop? Shall I overtake them?' And He answered, 'Pursue, for you shall overtake them and without fail recover all.'"*
> *—1 Samuel 30:8*

In life, we often experience great difficulties and challenges. When our lives become difficult, it is easy to forfeit and give up pursuing the life God has ordained for us. What should our attitude be when it appears we have lost in life rather than gained?

This question is answered in the life of David. David was a man after God's own heart and would eventually become the second king of Israel. He had incurred and suffered great loss at Ziklag as he hid from King Saul. He may have pondered if he was in the will of God for his life. It is the will of God to pursue, overtake, and recover all. This means we must have a tenacity to diligently accomplish everything God has ordained for us to have. In this pursuit, our demeanor should be that of an overtaker. No matter what difficulties or challenges we face, we have to ability to overcome and conquer them. After the conquest, we have the guarantee of complete recovery.

In this verse, the prophet Samuel chronicled the life of David, especially his journey being anointed as the second king of Israel and his ascension to the throne. While on the run for his life from King Saul, David became the leader of an unlikely group of men and settled in a country called Ziklag. As David and his men returned to

Ziklag, they discovered all their wives and children had been kidnapped. Their city had been ravaged and burned with fire. Many of the men began to weep, but David encouraged himself in the Lord, His God. David provides for us a picture of a Kingdom response to life's challenges. David asked God what he should do—should he go after their families, engage the enemy, and overtake them? God gave David the assurance he needed. God told him not only to pursue them, overtake them, but also he would recover all without fail.

Since God said it, we need to believe it; that settles it, and we will achieve it. Today is the beginning of your recovery. We have a guarantee from God Himself. Be encouraged and engage whatever challenge is before you. With God on our side, we have the confident expectation of complete success.

Day 19

A New Thing

> *"Do not remember the former things, nor consider the things of old. Behold, I will do a new thing, now it shall spring forth; shall you not know it."* —Isaiah 43:19

Many believers spend a lot of time thinking about our past. When we dwell so much on the past, it may cause us to live with regrets. None of us can change our past, but we can definitely learn from it.

No matter our current circumstances, God desires to do a new thing in our lives. God never repeats Himself. He wants to move us from faith to faith and from glory to glory. Our Father has things prepared for us to receive in this life more than we can imagine. His best life is waiting for us and is within our grasp.

In this verse, the prophet Isaiah wrote to encourage the nation of Israel. As a people, they experienced a difficult time in their lives. They had lost hope. They had become captives by one of their enemy nations. They had begun to feel like God had abandoned and forsaken them. Isaiah shared with the people that the Lord had commanded them not to remember the past. He did not want them to remember their past successes, victories, or conquests. God wanted them to know the new things which He had before them would be significant for them as He would establish them into a great people.

We have a guarantee from God about the new things He will establish and bring to pass in our lives. We must stop being so ensnared by our past and begin to recognize the new things right before our eyes. Release the past today and get ready for the new things.

Day 20

No Matter What, Still A Son

> *But the father said to his servants, "Bring out the best robe and put it on him and put a ring on his hand, and sandals on his feet. And bring the fatted calf here and kill it, and let us eat and be merry; for my son was dead and is alive again; he was lost and is found." And they began to be merry. —Luke 15:22-24*

It is difficult for many believers to embrace their true identity. We have permitted the world to define who we are. The adversary continues to bring havoc into our lives because we fail to know who we truly are to God through our relationship with Jesus Christ. We are not less than. We are not average. We are more.

We are uniquely and wonderfully made in the image and likeness of our Creator. We are just like God. His spiritual DNA resides in us. Even with our failures, we are still considered to be a son or daughter of God. We must embrace our sonship.

In this verse, Jesus Christ shared an important Kingdom principle. This parable was one of three parables that Christ taught to illustrate great spiritual truths. The so-called "religious leaders" often criticized Christ because He often communed with the least of society. In this parable, a man had two sons. The younger son, in his immaturity, came to his father and for his full inheritance. The younger son left the comfort and security of home and spent all he had on riotous living.

After all of his inheritance was depleted, he found himself in such a deplorable state, he desired to eat food for swine, but he came to himself. The younger son made a decision to return to his father after he acknowledged his sins. He thought in his mind that his father might receive him back as a servant. Christ concluded the parable by providing a picture of a loving father who had unconditional love and compassion for his son. The father gladly received his son back in his rightful place as a son no matter what he had done.

The father called for a great celebration by having his robe placed on him, a ring on his finger, and shoes on his feet. The son was celebrated and embraced as a son, no matter what he had done. This is a marvelous revelation of God's grace and mercy He extends to us no matter what sins we have committed. God wants us to embrace our rightful place as sons in the Kingdom of God. Let's began to live today as true sons and daughters of the King.

Day 21

Give Thanks in Everything

"Rejoice always, I pray without ceasing, in everything give thanks; for this is the will of God in Christ Jesus for you."
—1 Thessalonians 5:16-18

In our daily lives, we experience a multitude of things. We are not always able to prevent certain circumstances from happening to us, but we can always determine how we respond to them. We often respond with, "Why?" Especially if the circumstances are not what we wanted to happen.

However, as believers, our response should be to always give thanks in everything. When we pause and reflect on all we have received from God through Jesus Christ, it is easy to express our gratefulness. All we have or will ever have are gifts from our Heavenly Father.

In this verse, the Apostle Paul tells us how we are to give thanks. He wrote to the Thessalonian believers to encourage them to rejoice always. In addition, Paul told them to pray without intermission and in all things, give thanks. No matter what happens in our lives, we are to give thanks in every situation and circumstance. We clearly know God does not send evil and bad things into our lives, but He often permits them for a greater purpose.

If it is God-sent, then it will be God-used. Remember, the Father loves us, and He deserves our thanks in all things.

WEEKLY DEVOTIONAL REFLECTION QUESTIONS

1. What were the major spiritual truths revealed to you during this week?
2. What spiritual truths and/or principles can you apply to your spiritual life from this week's devotions?
3. How do you plan to share the spiritual truths and/or principles with others around you?

WEEK 4
DAYS 22-27

"Provisions in the Kingdom of God"

Day 22
"It Won't Work"

> *"'No weapon that is formed against thee shall prosper; and every tongue that rise up against thee in judgment that shalt condemn. This is the heritage of the servants of the Lord, and their righteousness is of me,' saith the Lord."*
> —Isaiah 54:17

We can always expect to be attacked by the enemy due to the anointing of God resting upon us. An indication of our increased favor with God will be Satan's attacks through man's futile attempt to derail our Kingdom assignment. We should become excited when we see a cadre of different weapons formed against us.

God often permits Satan to falsely accuse us or use slander, sickness, jealousy, hatred, conspiracy, or verbal attacks at the hands of family, friends, co-workers, and even members within the body of Christ. There is little we can do to prevent the weapon from being formed, but we can rejoice with this truth: it will not prosper, and it will not work.

In this verse, the prophet Isaiah wrote to the nation of Israel as they experienced a great time of ruin and captivity. The prophet released a word of encouragement to them as God prepared to restore them back to favor and prominence. He plainly told them the weapon would be formed, but it would not succeed in hurting or harming them. God also had given them the power to condemn the carrier of the weapon.

We must remember people are not our real enemies because we don't wrestle against flesh and blood. Since we are made in the image and likeness of God, we have the power in our mouths to condemn every carrier of the weapon being formed against us. God spoke through the prophet to remind them this is our covenant right as His servant. Our Heavenly Father will defeat every weapon formed against us because we are made righteous through Him. We no longer have to remain passive and live in defeat. It is time for us to open our mouths and use the Word of God as the sword of the Spirit to defeat every weapon being formed by our adversary. It won't work.

Day 23

Enter Into Rest

"Come to Me, all you who labor and are heavy laden, and I will give you rest." —Matthew 11:28

In the daily pressures of life, many of us often experience stress. If stress is not properly alleviated, it can become a robber of the abundant life promised to us by Jesus Christ. Stress occurs in our lives when we feel obligated to handle the pressures, pain, and persecution in life rather than allow Jesus Christ to handle them. We have a remedy for stress found in the Word of God.

What does it mean to enter into rest? It means to come to place of contentment and to cease from any movement of labor in order to recover and recollect one's strength. All of us are in need of this rest. God has provided us a way to enter into rest through Jesus Christ.

In this verse, Jesus Christ shared with His followers the secret to entering into rest. During this time, the Jewish religious leaders had placed enormous additional responsibilities on the people in the name of religion. These so-called "religious leaders" had added six hundred more precepts to the original law given to them from Moses. Jesus Christ was sent from God to move them as well as us from religion to relationship.

Unfortunately, the Jewish religious leaders rejected Jesus Christ and did not experience this rest. Jesus told them to come to Him and rest, especially if they were weary and burdened. Christ actually told them the system of religion would place heavy burdens on them. Religion often is centered on man-centered rules and regulations, programs and protocol, and the do's and don'ts. However, in the Kingdom of God, the primary focus is on Jesus Christ who is our Savior and having a personal relationship with Him as our King. **It is time for us to stop laboring, toiling, and stressing and make a decision to enter into rest. Let's Release Every Stress Today and be refreshed.**

Day 24

You Were Chosen Before

> *"Before I formed you in the womb, I knew you. Before you were born I sanctified you; I ordained you a prophet to the nations."* —Jeremiah 1:5

Each of us has been born with a pre-ordained destiny. Many of us focus solely on the journey in life, but have forgotten about our true destination in life. We have been uniquely and wonderfully made in the image and likeness of God for a great Kingdom purpose. Our God-ordained destiny is greater than we can think or imagine. Our lives consist more of the current problems and pain we may face today.

God chose us before the foundation of the world for a great destiny. As a matter of fact, God has completed our destiny before we were born. We have everything inside us to successfully complete our true purpose, but we often struggle with inadequacy and a lost knowledge of who we truly are.

In this verse, God spoke to the prophet Jeremiah about his Kingdom purpose. Jeremiah was keenly aware God had called him but was concerned if he could complete his assignment. God told Jeremiah before he had been conceived in his mother's womb, God was intimately aware of him and had set him apart as a prophet to the nations. The call on Jeremiah's life was not to be a prophet, but to be a prophet to the nations.

The Kingdom Moment

God has called all of us to great destiny. He intimately knows everything about us and everything that will happen in our lives, whether good or bad, but He does not disqualify us. God has made a commitment to us and has set us apart for a great work before time occurred. Remember, we were chosen before the foundation of the world and embrace our being chosen by God so we may accomplish we were created to do all in life.

Day 25
Killing the Spirit of Fear

"For God has not given us a spirit of fear, but of power and of love, and of a sound mind." —2 Timothy 1:7

What could we accomplish in our lives if we were not fearful? What dreams could we fulfill? What business could we start? What books could we write? Many believers are paralyzed in life because of fear. Fear is a robber of the *best* life God has ordained for us.

Some have said that the acronym for fear is, "false evidence appearing real." However, as believers, we have been called to walk a life of faith and not to be ruled by fear. In order to walk by faith, we must live our lives in agreement with the Word of God. Many of us have been become fearful because we have been the recipients of negative words spoken into our lives. We also may not have been nurtured and raised in a loving and supporting environment and it caused us to fear. The time has come for us to kill and slay this spirit of fear.

In this verse, the Apostle Paul wrote this letter to encourage his spiritual son, Timothy. Timothy was the pastor of the church at Ephesus. As a young pastor, he often struggled with inadequacy and not feeling fully equipped to lead and govern the church. Paul shared with him a powerful spiritual truth: we will not walk in the fullness and the greatness God has for us until we kill this spirit of fear. Paul told him he had not been given the spirit of timidity and cowardice, but he had been given power, strength, an ability to love, and a mind yielded to self-control.[5]

In order for us to kill this spirit of fear, we must have our minds renewed by the Word of God. We must make a decision to no longer live in fear, but to live a life of faith. Because of the indwelling power of God, we can live and love in His power. We can conquer and succeed in life because of His power. Begin to put fear under our feet where it belongs. Remove the "pause" button and go after all the promises of God.

---

[5] https://www.blueletterbible.org/lang/Lexicon/Lexicon.cfm?strongs=G4995&t=KJV

Day 26
Born to Rule

> *"Then God said, 'Let us make man in our image according to our likeness, let them have dominion over the fish of the sea, over the birds of the air, and over the cattle, over all the earth and over every creeping thing that creeps on the earth.'"*
> *—Genesis 1:26*

Many of us have settled to live an average life of mediocrity. However, it is God's desire for us to live the abundant life. Our God-ordained destiny is more than our daily rising of going to work, paying bills, returning back to home, going to bed, and repeating the cycle again every day. Inside each of us is an innate desire to do more and to be more in life. As a matter of fact, God has created us to rule and reign in life.

Being created to rule means we were created to live a life of dominion. Dominion in its simplest form means to rule over every circumstance, situation, and problem in life. Debt is not to rule us. Sickness is not to rule us. Poverty is not to rule us. Hatred is not to rule us. Racism, sexism, depression, anger, and unforgiveness are not to rule us.

In this verse, in the book of beginnings, Moses wrote about the biblical truth about rulership. God convened a meeting of His heavenly council and declared a decision to make man in their image and likeness. Mankind was created to be God's representative on the earth for dominion over the earth as God ruled the heavens. At this moment, we have the presence, purpose, plans, potential, and power of God inside us. We are born to rule. We are born for success. We are born to live a Kingdom-focused life.

It is time for us to awaken to our real identity and live the *best* life. There is a ruler in you. It is ruling time!

Day 27

God is a Healer

> *"God said, 'If you will diligently heed the voice of the LORD your God and do what is right in His sight give your ear to His commandments and keep all His statues, I will put none diseases on you which I brought on Egyptians. For I am the LORD who heals you.'"*
> *—Exodus 15:26*

Many of us are not living a blessed life because of sickness. It is the will of God to be whole in every area of our lives including our physical health. Unfortunately, we have many believers who are just as sick as non-believers. We live with sickness and even die prematurely from sickness. However, we must know and believe God is the ultimate healer.

There are many untruths about sickness we have been erroneously taught. Sickness is not from God and is not caused by God. Sickness is the result of the entrance of sin into the world. Some sickness is the result of unconfessed sin. Some sickness is the result of improper food diets. No matter what causes or permits sickness, we can have full confidence God heals.

In this verse, Moses and the nation of Israel had witnessed God's power first hand as they were led out of Egypt through the Red Sea on dry ground. After the nation of Israel safely passed through, God destroyed Pharaoh and all the Egyptians by drowning them. On their way to the Promised Land, the people began to complain and murmured against Moses because they needed drinking water. God told

Moses to take a tree branch, and he casted it into the waters. As the tree branch hit the waters, the waters became sweet. This is a picture and shadow of Jesus Christ. Jesus Christ died on a tree called Calvary and shed His blood for our salvation. With Christ's death on this tree and by His stripes, healing was provided for us.

God told Moses if the people of Israel would be obedient and keep His commandments, they would not have the sicknesses of the Egyptians placed upon them because He is the Lord who heals. This is a picture of a conditional covenant. Today, we have a better covenant through the finished work of Jesus Christ. We have a right to receive healing for all sickness and disease. It is free because Jesus has already paid the full price at the Cross. We have a promise from God for healing. Let's believe and receive our healing today!

WEEKLY DEVOTIONAL REFLECTION QUESTIONS

1. What were the major spiritual truths revealed to you during this week?
2. What spiritual truths and/or principles can you apply to your spiritual life from this week's devotions?
3. How do you plan to share the spiritual truths and/or principles with others around you?

WEEK 5
DAYS 28-31

"The Power of Praise"

Day 28

The Power of Praise

> *"And when he had consulted with the people, he appointed those who should sing to the Lord, and who should praise the beauty of holiness, as they went out before the army and were saying: 'Praise the Lord, for His mercy endures forever.'"* —2 Chronicles 20:21

We have been uniquely and wonderfully made in the image and likeness of God. Not only are we a speaking spirit like our Creator, but we also have this innate capacity to offer praise and worship. On a daily basis, we may give praise to people around us or may receive praise from them. Receiving praise from others often makes us feel better about ourselves.

There are several meanings of praise. Praise is the act of expressing admiration or approval. Praise is the ability to speak well about others. As believers, we understand the power of praise. When attacks come in our lives, it is Satan's desire for us to retreat, become isolated, and stop releasing praise to God. True and authentic praise is addressed to God and is a great weapon to thwart and stop the enemy's assault in our lives. We should praise God daily and at all times.

In this verse, we see this power of praise at work, and the successful outcome that came to King Jehoshaphat and the people of Judah. The king received word about an impending attack from his enemies. The king called a fast throughout the nation. He also began to remind God about His promises of protection and deliverance.

Jehoshaphat received instructions from the prophet of God about their strategy of protection. The king was instructed to place a group of singers before the army. As the group of singers began to praise God, God supernaturally intervened and caused their enemies to fight and kill each other.

When the king and his army came upon their enemies, they were already dead. It took them a total of three days to recover all the spoils from their enemies. The king and his people were tremendously blessed despite an eminent attack from their enemies. When the enemy attacks our lives, we have the victory in our mouths in the form of praise. We should never remain silent and quiet. We need to learn to boldly declare, "Praise the Lord, for His mercy endures forever." Praise is our weapon, and it is time to use it!

Day 29

Don't Worry, Be Happy

"Be anxious for nothing, but in everything by prayer and supplication, with thanksgiving, let your requests be made known to God." —Philippians 4:6

We will never experience a life of wholeness without peace in our minds. We often experience a lack of peace due to a misalignment of focus. Many believers have a daily battle for peace in their minds.

Many people worry. We are strangled with all of the pressures of life. Worry comes when the thoughts in our minds pulls us in different directions and tears us apart. A person who worries constantly thinks about their problems and never seeks God as the answer.

In this verse, the Apostle Paul gave the secret to the believers at Philippi on how to live a worry-free life. Paul admonished them not to be anxious about anything, but they were to bring everything to God in prayer. Many of us are anxious because we are troubled with cares of this world. God expects us to cast all of our cares upon Him because He cares for us. We need to pray to God about everything. Prayer is addressed to God and not to people. We must stop bringing our problems to people who also have their own problems. God wants us to bring our problems to Him; He is the answer and He has the answer.

Effective prayer begins with adoration of our Heavenly Father and also includes thanksgiving. We have so much to be thankful for.

The Kingdom Moment

Let's stop worrying today and learn to be happy. We must make a conscious decision to enjoy life in spite of our circumstances, challenges, and cares.

Day 30

Maximize Today

"And Jesus said to him, 'Assuredly, I say to you, today, you will be with Me in Paradise.'" —Luke 23:43

Each day we are granted a gift from God called today. Many people appear to put their lives on hold. Either we are ensnared by our past or anxiously await the arrival of the future. It is essential for us to learn to maximize today. We must move our deferred dreams from the shelf and relaunch them today. It is time to enroll in college today. Begin to write a book today.

Maximizing today means to make a decision to live our lives to the greatest possible degree. We will never experience the full blessings of God until we learn to live today. In order to maximize today, we must stop the thieves from robbing our quality of life—the thief of yesterday and the thief of the future.

In this verse, Luke recorded this conversation between Jesus Christ and the two thieves who hung on crosses with Him during the crucifixion. One thief told Jesus in Luke 23:39, "If you are the Christ, then save us and save yourself." Real faith for today is possible when we remove the all the "ifs" out of our lives.

The second thief told Jesus to remember him when He came into His Kingdom. The second thief represents the "future thief."

How did Christ respond? Jesus responded, "Today you will be with me in Paradise." This statement illustrates God is not bound by time-past or future- but lives in the dimension of today called *now*.

The Kingdom Moment

Make a decision to live today. Make a decision to love today. Make a decision to forgive today. Make decision to have faith today. We must not allow procrastination to cause us to stop doing the things we need to complete and do today. Today is a gift, and it is time to maximize it!

Day 31

Choose the Abundant Life

"The thief does not come except to steal, kill, and destroy. I have come that they may have life and that they may have it more abundantly." —John 10:10

God has granted us an opportunity to live the abundant life. However, the abundant life is evading many believers. We perish due to a lack of knowledge about the Word of the God and the personal application of the Word of God to our lives. Many of us have reserved the abundant life to be lived after we transition from this life and spend eternity with the Lord. There is no need to wait to begin to live the abundant life. We can choose the abundant life today.

We must make decision to stop embracing the traditions of men and began to embrace the truth of the Word of God. The abundant life is the life of God, which has been promised to us through our relationship with Jesus Christ. The abundant life is about the quality and quantity of life. The abundant life is the life of believers demonstrating the fullness of God in their lives, without anything broken, missing, or lacking.

In this verse, John recorded these words declared by Jesus Christ. Christ provided for His hearers and for us the real purpose of His coming into the world. He clearly stated the thief had come to reduce the quality and quantity of life, but He came to bring the abundant life. The thief in this context represents the teachers of traditions and not Satan. Often, it is the traditions of men that cause many of us to not experience this abundant life.

It is critical for us to choose the abundant life and leave the traditions of men. The choice is ours. Join me as I have chosen the abundant life!

WEEKLY DEVOTIONAL REFLECTION QUESTIONS

1. What were the major spiritual truths revealed to you during this week?
2. What spiritual truths and/or principles can you apply to your spiritual life from this week's devotions?
3. How do you plan to share the spiritual truths and/or principles with others around you?

SELECTED BIBLIOGRAPHY

Kariger, Brian, and Daniel Fierro. 1995. *Dictionary Reference*. May. http://dictionary.reference.com/.

Milligan, Jim, and Frank Rabinovitch. n.d. *Blue Letter Bible*. http://www.blbclassic.org/index.cfm.

ABOUT THE AUTHOR

Pastor Michael T. James, M.S. in Christian Ministry, is the senior pastor of Mount Vernon Missionary Baptist Church in Chapel Hill, TN.

He received a B.S. from Middle Tennessee State University in Murfreesboro, TN and a M.S. from Southern Christian University in Montgomery, AL. His post-graduate studies include certifications from Corporate Coach U-Licensed Facilitator, Vital Smart's Crucial Conversations-Licensed Facilitator, and various change management certificates. Pastor James is also a Toastmaster's International Certified Competent Communicator.

www.ingramcontent.com/pod-product-compliance
Ingram Content Group UK Ltd.
Pitfield, Milton Keynes, MK11 3LW, UK
UKHW022212230426
12048UKWH00016BA/807